FROM THE PEW TO THE PULPIT:
GOD'S PLAN

FROM THE PEW TO THE PULPIT:
GOD'S PLAN

Tyrone J. Pickett

From the Pew to the Pulpit: God's Plan
By Tyrone J. Pickett
Copyright © 2022 by Pickett Innovation

All rights reserved. No part of this book may be reproduced, distributed, or transmitted in any form or by any means, without the prior written permission of the publisher, except in the case of brief quotations embodied in critical reviews and certain other noncommercial uses permitted by copyright law.

Scriptures are taken from The Holy Bible King James Version (Public Domain) except where otherwise notated.

For permission requests, write to the publisher, addressed "Attention: Permissions Coordinator," at:
Pickett Innovation
373 Bronze Dr.
Rocky Point, NC 28457

First Edition: November 23, 2022
This book is an inspirational book of how God can take your life and turn it around. Man plans his way, but God directs his path.

ISBN#: 978-1-66641-495-0

NuVision Publishing
www.nuvisiondesigns.biz

Printed in the United States of America

TABLE OF CONTENTS

Chapter 1: Introduction 7

Chapter 2: God's Plan 9

Chapter 3: From the Pew to the Pulpit-The Calling .. 19

Chapter 4: Anger; Animosity; Resentment; Bitterness 27

Chapter 5: Training 29

Chapter 6: The Bleeding Heart of a Pastor 39

Chapter 7: A Man and His Mission 47

Chapter 8: Recognize the Potential 49

Final Chapter: From Glory to Legacy 51

From the Pew to the Pulpit
Tyrone Pickett

Chapter 1: Introduction

The best thing in my life happened when I was born in the year of 1975, June 5th. Not knowing that this birth was going to be an unusual one. It did not matter to me. I was destined to get here. I was born backwards, as I would say, but the correct medical term is "breech". Yes, that is right. My mother told me I was born a breech baby. A breech birth is when a baby is born bottom first instead of headfirst, as is normal. Around 3–5% of pregnant women at term (37–40 weeks pregnant) have a breech baby. Due to their higher-than-average rate of complications for the baby, breech births are considered higher risk. Being born breech should have been a sign that my life would be filled with challenges. Well, here I am, but here comes another challenge.

The doctor pronounced me dead according to my grandfather. Now this is a start if I have ever heard of one. Born breech, then the doctor pronounces me dead. But thanks be to God, He had a different plan. Well, you may say this story sounds familiar. It might just be because my life sounds like a lot of people whose life is filled with challenges. Let us move forward. I will come back and catch you up.

From the Pew to the Pulpit
Tyrone Pickett

My mom had me at an early age. She was thirteen, almost fourteen. Her mom passed when she was nine years old and my grandfather was raising her and three other siblings as a single parent. I thank God for my grandfather. Len would give me, along with my grandfather, consent to one of his sisters to help raise me. I consider myself a country boy, but I yearned to be a city boy, all because that's where my mother was. I never knew the struggle she had to face as a child having a child at such an early age.

So many years went by. I had a type of hurt and resentment towards my mom, not realizing my mother did the best thing that she could do for me. Through its twist and turns, life has a way of molding us into the person we are meant to become. Especially when you have misguided thoughts and no understanding of a person's life until you talk and have a conversation about the personal challenges they have had to overcome. Forty-seven years later, I can say that I have grown, understand, and learned that God's plan is better than our plan.

From the Pew to the Pulpit
Tyrone Pickett

Chapter 2: God's Plan

34°39'40"N and longitude 77°41'46"W, some would say, "What's this?" This is the place where it all happened for me, where I learned to become the son, leader, the husband, the father, the prayer warrior, worshipper, and Pastor that I am today. Momma Madie, who is my late Grandfather's sister, *tore my behind up* growing up. She was the type of woman who put the fear of God in you. I'll tell you more about that a little later. Well, she was given the opportunity to raise me. She told my grandfather "Boot," as he was affectionately called, that she would raise me for him. This opportunity unfolded because Aunt Madie did not believe in an abortion. That's right, it was a thought to have me aborted. Remember I said life has challenges. She accepted the challenge even though she had lost her youngest child, Walter, at the age of 12. I came into her life to fill a void. God has a way of doing things. To be exact, his name was Walter Jackson Holmes, and would you know it? I have part of his name: Tyrone Jackson Pickett. His name reminds me of the struggle she faced even in raising me with the hurt and thought of a lost child. But I feel somehow God placed me here for her, and her here for me.

Momma didn't play any games with me growing up.

From the Pew to the Pulpit
Tyrone Pickett

She always loved to cook, sew, quilt, can food, and help others. She sowed every seed she had into me and my brothers/cousins. Growing up in the house as the baby had its benefits. But also, it had its disappointments. There were times where I could not go where I wanted to go or hang out with my friends who I thought were my friends at that time. All because I was the baby, and I was guarded by a mother who had suffered loss. Growing up I didn't realize she was suffering that way. God revealed it to me years later when I had these questions and I asked Him. I asked God, "Why it seems like Momma never let me do anything?" I had a neighbor who I would say was a close friend of mine. We lived, I mean, right next door, but Momma told me I could go as far as to the ditch. Well, I went to the ditch, and we played catch from one side of the ditch to the other. Now granted, I see now that Momma wasn't that strict. She was protecting the gift God had given her.

There were times when my biological Mom would visit me. Momma would let me go and spend time with her. Even one time I remember going to DC with my grandfather riding on his Winnebago. Good memories I have of those times. There were times growing up when we went to DC to visit. I remember the time when

From the Pew to the Pulpit
Tyrone Pickett

I was there on 36th St. I went to the playground playing football, this guy pushed me down, and I ended up getting cut on my knee. My grandfather mended my wound. Well, I remember him getting the band-aid. All of this had part of me growing up to who I am today. My grandfather made the decision to give me to my Great-Aunt to be raised, and for that I am grateful. The funny thing is that growing up I would call my grandfather Uncle Boot. I did not realize at an early age that he was my grandfather. You learn lessons in life and you take heed. Family kept secrets. But it wasn't a secret. It was all on God's timing when the truth would come to fruition. The early years of my life I dealt with challenges of hurt, rejection, abandonment, and loss. Someone might say, "Wow, after all of that, how did you make it through?" Follow me along this journey. My life isn't like Moses. It is like being raised in another house and not knowing that God is going to raise you up for His people.

I had to be delivered from a mental stronghold over my life. Mental (relating to the Mind) Strongholds: a place that has been fortified to protect it against attack, a place where a particular cause or belief is strongly defended or upheld. I had to learn to think and speak positive. Negative talk and thinking can eat you up like a cancer. Proverbs 23:7 (KJV) *For as he thinketh in his heart, so is he: Eat and drink, saith he to thee; but his heart is not with thee.* My mind had to be positive, but I was caught in the cycle of family let down. Put on positive qualities. Put away negative qualities. I found two key words that were repeated several times in many of the scripture verses that will follow in these other articles. Those two key words are "putting on" and "putting away." The Bible tells us that we are the ones who are to try and "put on" the good and godly qualities that God will want us to have operating in our personalities, and to "put away" all the bad and negative qualities that He will not want us to have operating in our personalities. Many people are missing it. They have been walking with the Lord for years and they wonder why there has not been many changes in the very cores of their personalities. Where is the love, joy, peace, sound mind, and self-control that the Bible promises me once I fully commit my life to the Lord? I had to learn that this is the will of God for your life that you let Him enter you into a sanctification process in order that He may fully consecrate you to Himself and start to mold, shape, and transform you into the express image of His Son Jesus Christ.

"Caught in the cycle of family let down", today as I sit

here writing, I am reviewing my past and how I was reared. See, my mother was never in my life and I am now grown. I am still having issues with the type of relationship that I and my mother have. Often, I look for her to be there in support as she says she will be. Once again, I find myself confronting the lingering effects of abandonment, even at the age of 38. How often I wish that life was so different than in the way that it has been mapped out for me. However, I realize God makes no mistakes, but I wonder why we as people keep making the same mistakes over again. Maybe my mistake is trusting too much in someone who seems to keep letting you down. Often too many promises are made, and once again too many promises are not kept.

> **I keep telling myself not to allow them to get close to me again, but how is it that I keep letting them back in?**

It's hard at times because you cannot choose who your heart will love. All I ever wanted in my life is to feel like I have a place to belong. This has been my spiritual struggle in life. How can I stop from getting my heart broken from those who are supposed to be the closest to me? I find myself occupying my time with many

From the Pew to the Pulpit
Tyrone Pickett

desires or things just to distract my mind to keep my heart from getting so involved with people. Alternately, I tend to involve myself in people's lives, attempting to help them achieve the very things that I have wanted for myself. I realize that there is no perfect family. In life we always look for approval from mommy or daddy. But what happens when the approval is only lip service? Maybe I am looking for too much from them. Maybe I expect too much in my life at this point. **I feel the hurt of so many people who have walked in my shoes and the hurt of those who are still walking in my shoes.** I look for my life to be fulfilled by acceptance. I look for my father's approval. I look for my mother's approval. Even though I know who they are, and where they are, I still feel like I am alone. Charge it not to my heart, but I can't help to feel what my heart has gone through for so many years. I try to camouflage my feelings. But I don't even know what to feel anymore. I don't know how to even care anymore.

"God, I ask you to heal me from my past. I ask you to destroy this yoke off my life so that I can walk completely free in this life without those feelings of bondage anymore."

How many times has your heart been broken? I have

From the Pew to the Pulpit
Tyrone Pickett

been looking for a way of escape. I have been looking for outlets for my mind to not have to focus so much on the disappointing times I have had in my life, and it seems like sometimes it keeps taking me in a cycle. I am tired of going through the same issues, or dealing with the same problem, of just not being able to trust people. Its seems that the most hurt comes from those who are supposed to be so close to you. I am tired of being hurt. I am tired of hurting. I have learned how to hide through my emotions from different situations in my life. But what happens when you stop trying to have emotions? What happens when you try not to allow your feelings to get involved with people? It seems as if we keep going through the valley. I want to write new memories in my life to replace the memories of my life that were negative. But it seems as if the memories that keep surfacing are the ones of my past. No time has changed anything. No cycle has been broken. It is still ongoing.

"God, please help me to get off this roller coaster of life."

I have new goals I have set for my life, but once again it seems as I have no one to share my accomplishments with in my life. It bothers me that my

From the Pew to the Pulpit
Tyrone Pickett

mom wasn't there to meet my extended family. What's an accomplishment in your life without your family there to help you celebrate different milestones? What is a birthday party without anyone there to help you enjoy it? **This has been my dilemma.** I have missed so many memories without being able to share them with my family. Sometimes I feel like I have been cheated, not by God, because God is too wise to make any mistakes. But just by life sometimes. Here is my heart on page. I celebrate to wrap myself around people that I feel that love me, but even yet some of the most important ones forget the very day I was born.

"God help me. I feel like I am going in another cycle. I am thankful for life. I am thankful for the life that has been given, but God I am now ready to live my life to the fullest."

I realize that writing is my outlet. I have often written poetry to express how I feel. Now I realize that there is so much more in me to write to explain, to remove the bondage of my life and to express to others who have been on this same cycle in life who may be experiencing the same heartfelt issues or dealing with this same cycle of life. I have gone to school. I have become successful. God has prospered me to reach goals in my life. God has always been there. "But God I also wanted my Dad and Mom to have been there. I know that this seems selfish on my part. God, I know you know the pain of separation from your son, who, in carrying out your will, entered human history to redeem humankind from the severance brought about by sin, bridging the chasm it created in your love for us. God, I am sure you can relate in the attribute of being God the Son, in the garden of Gethsemane agonizing to just wanting to make the Father happy of completing the assignment that Daddy had given you. God, I know you can relate to how it felt to have been rejected by the one who was supposed to be the closest to you. I know you can understand what it feels like to have been put aside for others. I realize from studying your word that this has been a cycle for a while now. How can we deny your love that you have for us? I don't understand how my parents could deny the love that I have for them, and the question I ask myself is how we can deny the love that you have for us?"

Chapter 3: From the Pew to the Pulpit - The Calling

Years have passed by since I first thought about being a Pastor. I was young and I was raised by my great-aunt who is my Mom that raised me. Growing up, she taught us to pray at 5:00am in the morning and study the Bible. I never realized that she was preparing me for ministry. She taught me a lot about studying God's Word and understanding what the Bible really meant and means to explaining God's Word. I remember pretending to be a preacher in my Mom's prayer room. This room started out as a garage that my Mom turned into her prayer room. But let's go back a few years to where it all begins.

See, my biological Mom was very young when she gave birth to me. My Aunt Madie took me in her home and promised God that she would raise me so I would not have to run from pillar to post. She raised me because she loved my Mom and my Grandfather. She wanted to help my Mom get on her feet without worrying about her child and for her to know that I was in good hands.

Several miracles took place in my life. The first one was when I was born and the doctor pronounced me dead,

From the Pew to the Pulpit
Tyrone Pickett

according to my Grandfather, Boot. My Grandfather is now deceased, but he made sure that I knew what God had done in my life.

My childhood was like any other child growing up, but I noticed certain things a little differently than my friends from the neighborhood, and even some of my classmates. I started looking at my friends and noticing that they looked like their parents. There were similarities. They either looked like their Mom or their Dad. There were some differences but I noticed that there were some similar features and resemblances.

I wondered why I didn't look like my Dad or my Mom?

> **Identity: What is my identity? Who do I look like? I don't see it. I look in the mirror. I don't have my Dad's eyes. I don't have my Mom's nose. His ears don't look like mine. I don't have his smile. I don't have her cheekbones. Who am I? Who do I belong to?**

Those questions continued to cry out as I grew older and the more I looked in the mirror. There's something deep inside of me that I can't relate to. I need answers. *"God, who am I? Sitting outside on the porch looking at the sun going down and tears rolling down my face. I have questions but how do I get the answers?"*

Little did I know answers would soon come. There was a knock at the door. "Who is it?", I replied. "Boot," the man said. My Uncle Boot had come into town to visit my Mom. He always came by our house when he was visiting from Washington, DC. Well, during this time my Grandmother was sick. We were on our way to the hospital to check on her. We all rode in his camper (Winnebago) to the hospital. While we were riding in the camper, I remember getting a Canada Dry Ginger Ale out of the refrigerator. This is the reason I like Ginger Ale today. Those small memories set seeds in my mind of my childhood. Moving on.

We went to check on Grandma Rebecca. We got a phone call saying, "Grandma isn't doing too well." We all rush to the Hospital. I saw people that I didn't know. And then, my Grandma passes. My Grandma actually dies. I was very upset. I ran behind the house and begin to break down crying. I was close to my grandmother. She kept me near to her and now she's gone. But something is wrong. I can't put my finger on it, but something is wrong. A lot of people are arguing.

From the Pew to the Pulpit
Tyrone Pickett

What in the world is going on?

Wait...someone just got cut. Uncle Boot, somebody cut Uncle Boot. Who cut Uncle Boot? Wait...there's fighting going on. What in the world? Why are they fighting? There is some scuffle, some tussle, and it all comes out. What? Uncle Boot is not really my uncle? He's my Granddaddy. Who's my? Who's my? What? Wait! Can someone tell me what is going on? It has now all come out during my grandmother's funeral. It just so happened that I'm in a place and hearing things I had never known. It took the death of my grandmother for me to find out why I was having these negative feelings. There was more to my life than I realized.

Challenges

Some of my challenges were dealing with rejection. Rejection includes fear of rejection and self-rejection in this common demonic family. Beyond the inherited sins of our ancestors, rejection is typically the first doorway the enemy uses to attack. Tragically, due to parental influence, this assault can begin even in the womb. Rejection is one of the biggest problems of humans!

Rejection is defined as reject, refuse, repudiate, decline, deny, rebuff, repel, renounce, discard, throw away, exclude, eliminate.

From the Pew to the Pulpit
Tyrone Pickett

Have you had these feelings before? Rejection is very common among Christians. What we call love often pales beside the love of God. But when God loves through us, it unleashes a power beyond our understanding. There seemed to be a cloud over my mind that says God does not love me anyway which caused me not to receive the revelations of truth. I was looking for love from anyone or anything because I was starving for the true love of Jesus. Because of past hurts and mistakes from others, it gave me a sense of unbelief and doubt towards the truth. It also let the spirit of hatred and bitterness come into my heart. I could not see rejection working in me. The trauma of rejection from my childhood had seared my mind over the truth. I spoke and allowed people to speak negative things about me. Because I could not see or receive the full love of Jesus, I could not love myself. Being rejected had me acting out in anger and even rage at times because I was subconsciously mad at God.

Being called by God comes with challenges, to say the least. A lot of my challenges prepared me to minister to people that I never knew I would have to minister to one day. One of the challenges I faced was dealing with the fact that I was raised without my mother and my father in my life. Yes, I had a family that loved me

From the Pew to the Pulpit
Tyrone Pickett

and raised me as their own. But growing up, I had seen other kids with their moms and dads. I never realized this until one day I found out that my Mom was not my real Mother and that my Dad was not really my Father. They were my great-aunt and great-uncle. To learn something at that age was a challenge that I faced and could not understand at the time why I was the one who had to be given away to be raised by someone else. I faced the challenge of rejection, feeling as if something was wrong with me. I faced challenges of other kids saying that their dads were this or their moms were that. For a long time, I dealt with the spirit of abandonment even though I knew had loving parents (guardians). Even still, there was still a void in my life. I had questions but had no answers. I would look in the mirror wondering who I looked like. I wondered if I had my Dad's eyes or my Mom's nose.

These challenges that I faced in life were preparing me to help Pastor a generation of people who would have the same questions 10-15-20 years later. At the time, I never knew. But God had a plan. What you choose to think about and dwell on in this life will make or break you as to what type of person you will end up becoming. Leave it to God the Father to perfectly capture, in one simple one-line sentence from the

From the Pew to the Pulpit
Tyrone Pickett

Bible, the secret to being able to have good mental health in this life.

Fast forward some years to childhood and it begins with me alone for a while. Then comes along other siblings: my biological brother and a cousin who we were all raised like natural brothers and sisters. I now realize that I had a younger brother. My baby brother to be exact. His name is James. He's two years younger than me. I now have someone to play with that I know I am close to. Me and my brother were very close growing up playing in the fields and in the woods. We also rode bikes and learned to build bow and arrows out of reeds and tree branches. Every morning, we had to start out with prayer and a bible scripture. If nothing else, my Mom, that I had recently learned was my Great Aunt Madie, taught us to learn to pray and study the word of God. You could call us the three from *Madie's Boot Camp.* Boot camp consisted of learning how to sew, cook, and make quilts. I must say for a long time it was me alone getting all the Boot Camp privileges. This training I realized years later prepared me for my calling as a Pastor. The training taught me how to serve. Serving in my community, serving others, and serving God. Many times, we learned to take care of others who were less privileged. During those

From the Pew to the Pulpit
Tyrone Pickett

Christmas seasons I learned to sew clothes for other people and learned to make quilts to give away during the holidays. This was preparing me for ministry, never knowing what God had in store for my life. There were times I regretted having to learn to do these things because none of my friends were doing them. I felt like I was being neglected and not allowed to have fun like my friends because I was always doing things that seemed to be outside of what other kids were doing. My Mom later told me that she was preparing me to survive on my own if I never got married.

Chapter 4: Anger; Animosity; Resentment; Bitterness

A short fuse, and a bad temper.
Challenges continued to follow me. I was looking for love in all the wrong places trying to buy love at an early age. I desired to be wanted and loved. I seemed to find myself getting hurt repeatedly. This challenge I faced began to build up anger and resentment inside of me. I felt as if I was not worthy to be loved. Because if my own father and mother didn't want me, then how could anyone else desire to love me? But little did I know, I did not have the complete story of how I got to where I was and did not have both sides. Years would come later where I would sit down with my biological Mom, sit down with my Father, and talk about what happened. But before we get there, let me share about how I found one of my callings God had for me.

For years I sang in the choir. For years I was in the background, but one day during rehearsal the idea came up for me to sing a song. I was nervous when first asked. But I volunteered to do it anyway. I will never forget that Sunday. I can't remember the song right now, but I remember singing the song and the Holy Spirit fell on me to the point that I started crying. After I had sang the song, this Deacon or Elder, I

From the Pew to the Pulpit
Tyrone Pickett

believe at the time, Rev. Floyd Holmes, stood up and asked, "Could I sing that song one more time?" After I sang the song again, he came and gave me three dollars. I was shocked and surprised that someone would ask me to sing this song and pay me three dollars to sing it. This was the first touch of the Holy Spirit on my life when I recognized that God had His hands on me. I continued to sing in the choir when we attended the church, but God was moving on my Mother's heart to start attending another ministry.

Chapter 5: Training

We left St. Paul Holiness church and began to attend Victory Deliverance Temple. There is where I began to get more training, not knowing God once again was preparing me for ministry. I began to learn how to set up the sanctuary for church, folding chairs and unfolding chairs, passing out fans and picking up fans after the church service was over. I also began to learn how to play the drums, sing more and how to direct the choir. Years of training went on in my life, from my teen years until I graduated and left my community to pursue my young adult life. I learned how to become a deacon during this time, being the first one to get to church to turn on the heat or the AC. I was taught that the Deacon should be the first one to get to church before a service and the last one to leave. I find myself still walking in those principles as a Pastor. Because no matter what title you have, we are to serve God's people. It's not about the title, but it's all about serving.

Years progressed on and I left my little community, but everything I learned stuck with me even when I moved to Washington, DC. I moved to DC to pursue two things: to fill the void of knowing my parents, and to further my education in college. But there were more challenges I would face. Having freedom comes with a

From the Pew to the Pulpit
Tyrone Pickett

price when you don't realize what freedom is. I thought I wanted to have a life where I could do what I wanted to do and go and come when I wanted to. But I was taught a valuable lesson at the age of 19.

June 5th, 1994. I was in Business College and was pursuing my career as an Electronic Technician. It was my birthday and I was going to be partying. I had worldly influence in my life I had never had before. I had freedom I had never had before. At the age of 19, I almost died from drinking too much because of the freedom I thought I wanted. It almost costed me my life.

Years later I was involved in a situation where I was working for a law firm at the time, but family challenges came up and I was involved in a situation where I was facing 15 years in prison. Still, I did not know God had His hands on me. Years passed where the opportunity was afforded to me to come back home to NC. I took the first thing smoking to get back to the Carolinas. But before that I heard the voice of the Lord speak to me and told me that my blessings were in North Carolina. A place I did not want to be, but that's where my blessings were. In 1998, I moved back to North Carolina around the summertime. I moved back home to help take care of my Dad/Great Uncle who was

From the Pew to the Pulpit
Tyrone Pickett

Momma Madie's/Great Aunt's husband who had Alzheimer's. I helped to take care of him until he passed around October. Two years later I was still acting like I didn't hear God's plan. I was back drinking and drugging and hanging out in the streets. I was still attending church, but I was a backslider. I tell you the favor of God was on my life. I had worked at a place called Thorn Apple Valley. Long story short, I got in a fight and lost the job. I was in the streets trying to sell drugs, hanging on the corner. I lived at my late cousin Debbie Jean's house because I knew better than to try that at my Momma's house. Two phone calls came to my Momma Madie's house. One to tell her that whatever I was doing on the street I needed to stop it because they were watching me. Another call came later telling me that a job placing agency called *Manpower* called me about a job at Leslie-Locke.

GOD'S HAND WAS TRULY UPON MY LIFE.

I went to take a urinalysis test to start the job. All I know is that God had to clean me up, because I know the state I was in from that weekend before. Time passes by and I'm working and I am invited to a Prayer group on the job by these women: Mother Esther, Teresa Williams, and Corinthian Simpson. These women were true Evangelists doing the work of the Lord. Teresa Williams invited me to come to her church and even

From the Pew to the Pulpit
Tyrone Pickett

said she would pick me up for church. I thought that was funny and that she must not have known where I was from. I told her that there were 7 churches on my street alone. She told me they must not have what I need because I wasn't going. Now, remember I had a home church, Victory Temple. I would go, but one Sunday I went with Teresa to church to Believer's Outreach. I met Pastor Ricky Bordeaux and his wife and the church family of Believer's Outreach. That Sunday I felt something like I had never felt before. I went back to my home church that following Sunday and rededicated my life to Christ.

Well, fast forward, I ended up marrying Teresa Williams, now Teresa Pickett. The way it happened was that I was cutting the grass one day, and I heard a voice tell me that she was my wife. Because I always believed in talking to God, I asked Him, "Was she my wife?" and He answered yes, "But the same way I blessed her with you is the same way I take her from you if you don't do what I called you to do." Twenty-two years later, fourteen years of ministry, and thirteen grandkids later, I am still following God's Plan. So, here's more about me.

From the Pew to the Pulpit
Tyrone Pickett

My name Tyrone J. Pickett is a spirit-filled preacher of the Gospel of Jesus Christ. I accepted his call to ministry at the age of twenty-one. A native of Maple Hill, NC, I graduated from Pender High School. On May 22nd, 2008, based upon the recommendations of the late Bishop C. E. Anderson, Sr., I was installed as an Elder and was installed as the Interim Pastor of Cornerstone Temple C.O.G.I.C. After a year of serving in the role of Pastor, it was talked over with Supt. Thomas Wiggins of the Greater Wilmington District and the members of Cornerstone Temple to decide if they wanted me to become their Pastor. After a unanimous vote, it was decided that I would become the Pastor. It was also decided that I needed to set up a name for the new ministry. The name that God placed in my heart was the Bread of Life Deliverance C.O.G.I.C. (The BOLD Church) affectionately called was birthed on May 22nd, 2009. I became the Pastor and Founder at the age of 34. I have also set up a radio broadcast with the help of my good friend and Mentor Pastor Robert Blackwell called *"I Have Something to Say"* which has been heard in 25 countries throughout the world.

I am now an Apostle in the Lord's church as well as an accomplished IT Professional Architect, specializing in

From the Pew to the Pulpit
Tyrone Pickett

Security and Forensics. I currently live in Rocky Point, NC, and have been married for twenty-two years to my wonderful wife, Teresa Pickett, where we serve in leadership as Pastors together. I serve as the Senior Pastor of the Kingdom Connection Church Ministries where I am the Senior Leader of the fellowship and Kingdom movement. For years I have worked and built two ministries in my 10 years of Pastorship. The First ministry being the Bread of Life Deliverance C.O.G.I.C "The BOLD Church." I am also working to establish and build "The House of Abraham Resource Center", "The Impact Alliance" and the newly established fellowship. Out of the fellowship the decision was decided to change the name of the Ministry to Kingdom Connection Church Ministries which was birthed on June 3rd, 2016, where it united three ministries into one, under one umbrella for the Kingdom. Through the teaching from my early childhood, I've won numerous awards for Public Speaking, Developing Technical Documentation, and Leading to Win Leadership Awards. Something I did not mention is that I found my outlet in poetry and became a distinguished Poet, and Worship Leader. God's plan continues to help mentor and develop people around me with the giftings and talents of God.

From the Pew to the Pulpit
Tyrone Pickett

My children helped ground me in the things of God as well, and I owe it to them and my wife Lady Teresa Pickett, and our four children: Sasha Smith, Crystal Williams, Tyree Smith, and Tyron Smith. Currently, I am in another season of my life equipping them for the works of ministry helping to groom and grow 13 churches, known as our grandchildren: 7 grandboys- Xavion, BJ, Nathan, Elijah, TJ, Josiah, Mycah, and 6 granddaughters Paisley, Aliyah, Zurrie, Zomoriah, Harmony, Melody. God has certainly laid His hands on my life and my ministry.

The House of Abraham Resource Center
The vision of the House of Abraham Resource Center is to reach the whole man: mind, body, and soul of our youth today and how to be an influential part of their community by teaching them how to become business minded. We give them tools and instruct them how to make the effort in furthering their education and succeeding. Also, the House of Abraham Resource Center is working on establishing a Youth Center in the Big City of Burgaw.

Impact Alliance
This personal ministry was set up in November 2012. The ministry helps to teach, build, and equip other men

From the Pew to the Pulpit
Tyrone Pickett

or women of the clergy by encouraging them with the Word of God, being a mentor, brother, and spiritual support to Pastors, Elders, and Ministers alike who deal with the calling of being a Pastor, Elder, Minister, or Deacon. Years of ministry has helped which include being the 1st Administrative Assistant of the East Coast Restoration District and being installed as the Bishop of Protocol for the Worker's Together in Christ Fellowship of Churches (WTIC) out of Capital Heights, MD on July 12, 2014. Truly God's plan has given me opportunities to even co-authored a book entitled *"Dad's Willing to be Dad's"*. **From the Pew to the Pulpit** also helped me to even do a Digital Broadcast that has been heard around the world in Malaysia, the Philippines, France, Canada, South Africa, United Arab Emirates, Mexico, and the United States on whope101.org Radio Broadcast *"I Have Something to Say"*. The mission for my life is the mandate according to, *Ephesians 4:12-16 (ESV) "To Equip the saints for the work of the ministry, for the building up the body of Christ, until we all attain the unity of the faith and of the knowledge of the Son of God, to mature manhood, to the measure of the stature of the fullness of Christ, so that we may no longer be children, tossed to and from by the waves and carried about by every wind of doctrine, by human cunning, by craftiness in deceitful* *schemes. Rather, speaking the truth in love, we are to grow up in every way into him who is the head, into Christ."*

Finally, after getting over the hurt, the rejection, and the resentment, I could now move forward in the gifting of an Apostle that was on my life. After careful consideration and much prayer and devotion, the decision was made to walk in Apostolic gift. I took counsel with Apostle Chris Tyson for three years about the burden on his heart. On September 26, 2021, I was affirmed as an Apostle in the Lord's Church under leadership of Apostle Chris Tyson, Sr. of the Bethel Fellowship of Covenant churches, headquarters found in Suitland, MD. Now, after all the challenges and the struggles, I realized that it has all helped me and helps me to build, develop, cultivate, and mentor other Pastors, Ministries, and fellowships throughout the Kingdom of God. **From the Pew to the Pulpit.**

Chapter 6: The Bleeding Heart of a Pastor

In the face of so many adversities, I often wonder about the struggle of my life. I realize that my childhood prepared me for the life that was ahead of me. It is often a misconception about the life of a Pastor, and a Christian's Journey. This struggle is not easy. Sometimes you feel like you are on the edge and often you feel like you are pushed over the edge. This is not by the people you don't trust. This is from the people you break bread with on a constant basis. But it amazes me that no one invests more into you than you invest in yourself. So, this is a new era for me to realize that I am no longer going to live for anyone except myself. I have always had a problem of loving myself growing up. But it took a dramatic situation to happen in my life to realize people talk a good game. But at the end of the day, you only want to deal with real soldiers, real players who have been dealing with the struggle on the same level that you have been.

It's hard being black, it's hard being big, it's hard being a Pastor. And here I am with those three strikes in my life. People say this and quote that, but it's only what they feel they should say to be spiritually or politically correct. Here I have been trying to figure out life for a long time, and it has come with many classroom

From the Pew to the Pulpit
Tyrone Pickett

experiences. Life is a school of hard knocks. It really is a hard knock life, and to me it seems like the knocks are getting even harder. But to me it's the way I look at life. Sometimes I look through other people's eyes from their testimonies of what they have confessed. But here I am now understanding that it was my wife I told before God, life or death, for better or worse. My marriage has taken a hit. My family has taken a hit, and I keep on moving like I don't feel the bleeding, or I act like I don't see the blood running from my heart. I move like I don't feel my lungs gasping for its last breath. But here I am back to the street mentality. I don't believe God ever intended for a lot of things to happen. We have been told to handle things this way or handle things that way. Was the information born out of the struggle, or was it given without ever having gone through it? People always have good advice when they haven't played the hands that you have been dealt. Life is filled with so many struggles. Struggles in the family, struggles in the church, struggles in the homes, struggles on the job. Struggles in your personal mind. People say, "I got your back," but do people really know what that means? It's more than words. So, don't say, "I got your back," until you have walked a couple of miles in my shoes.

From the Pew to the Pulpit
Tyrone Pickett

I see that even though I have been free, I allowed myself to be bound by circumstances. Years of me believing in something I wasn't even sure about. I was unsure about every step. Even to the point that I just kept walking, believing, and having faith that surely this was my destiny. But was this my destiny? Was this God's plan for me? Did I miss it? I know His Word says that all things work together for the good of those that love Him and are called according to His purpose. My question is, "Was this His purpose?" There's a big difference in purpose and God's Will. What happens when you lose your sanity or you lose your hope? What happens when you put your heart all in? I know why the scripture says guard your heart with all diligence (constant and earnest effort to carry out what is undertaken; persistent exertion of body or mind, the degree of care and caution required by the circumstances of a person) for out of it are the issues of life. I can't keep living a lie. I have lost my passion and I am tired of the whole idea of Pastoring anymore. My heart is no longer in it. I don't believe and I know it's not healthy. *3 John 1:2 (KJV) says, "Beloved, I wish above all things that thou mayest prosper and be in health, even as thy soul prospers."*

When it comes to ministry there are a lot of things that

From the Pew to the Pulpit
Tyrone Pickett

are uncertain. You are never prepared for being rejected. You are never prepared for being denied, and you are never prepared for being betrayed. It seems that a lot of times we think that when we left the world, we would not have to meet any of the things that we dealt with in the world. But that is the contrary.

In the world, things are not as hidden as it is in the church. Sunday after Sunday you deal with all types of individuals. Those that are broken, those that are looking for answers, those that are at their wits' end, those that want a closer walk with God, those that come out of obligation, those that come for the mere fact of saying that they came to church, and there are those who just come to be noisy. But I have also run into a types who are leeches, blood suckers, spiritual suckers, and financial suckers. Those who give you a sad love song, about how bad they need help or a played-out melody of why nobody will help them. I have come to the realization that everyone is in some sort of crisis: physically, mentally, financially, or spiritually. We find that we are trying to live a life without instructions or ideas of who we are or what we are to become. It seems as if we are in a marathon of our lives. We are trying to figure out where we run and how fast do we run. What is the track going to be like? Do I run fast

From the Pew to the Pulpit
Tyrone Pickett

here? Do I slow down here? When do I stop and take a break? It seemed easy when we first started out on this journey, never understanding that there would be pain on this journey and never coming to the knowledge of the things that we would have to face in life. We said, "Yes," to a lot of things, but pain was never intended to be one of them. Nobody likes pain. Nobody likes to have to deal with hurt, mischief, anxiety or the hurt of a scar or even a bleeding heart. But I have learned that God wants to take the pain and use it. He wants to take the hurt and use it. I asked God, "How you will use this?" He said that, "It will be used for my glory." I ponder on that word *Glory*. "You will use this for your Glory? The very thing that has hurt me? The very thing that has seemed to almost take my last breath? You envision that this would be for your glory. God tell me how this would be for your Glory?" First, he told me to look up the word *Glory*.

> *Glory is defined as: a very great praise, honor, or distinction bestowed by common consent; renown: something that is a source of honor, fame, or admiration; a distinguished ornament or an object of pride, adoring praise or worshipful thanksgiving, resplendent beauty or magnificence, a state of great splendor, magnificence, or prosperity; a state of absolute*

happiness, gratification, contentment, the splendor and bliss of heaven; heaven, to exult with triumph; rejoice proudly, obsolete, to boast, Glory be to God (used to express surprise, elation, the time of greatest achievement, popularity, success, or the like.

Now, He said, "Remember what Moses asked for? He asked me to show him My Glory, and I told him that no one has looked upon My Glory and lived, and the reason why no one has looked upon My Glory and lived is because of the things it takes to have My Glory placed upon you." It takes a death to everything of yourself, and nothing living but God.

Exodus 33:22, "When my glory passes by, I will put you in a cleft of the rock and cover you with my hand until I have passed by."

And so, I stand—wounded, weary, yet still walking. Not because I have the strength, but because His hand still covers me in the cleft of the rock. I've bled in silence, preached through heartbreak, and carried burdens that few could ever see. But now I understand: the bleeding heart of a pastor is not a sign of weakness—it's the evidence of divine surgery. God does not waste pain.

From the Pew to the Pulpit
Tyrone Pickett

He repurposes it for glory.

This chapter of my life may be written in tears, but it's sealed in triumph. I may not have chosen every battle, but I choose to rise. I choose to heal. I choose to love again—even if it begins with loving myself. Because if His glory demands death to self, then let this bleeding be the proof that something sacred is being born. I'm not done. I'm just being reshaped. And if this is what it takes to see His glory, then let the blood speak. Let it testify. Let it worship.

Chapter 7: A Man and His Mission

Mission: a sending or being sent for some duty or purpose; those sent. Also called foreign mission: a group of persons sent by a church to carry on religious work, especially evangelization in foreign lands, and often to establish schools, hospitals.

I realized by being in ministry, being a husband and a father that God had a mission for my life. I was reminded in the Bible about Daniel and I knew it was time to take a stand once and for all. There were some things in my life that had to be torn down: pride, rejection, hatred, and unforgiveness. These were images that were not of God and I could no longer allow them to dictate my life or take rule over me.

My mission focus was to be more like Christ. It took a lot for me to learn and I am still learning. The word came to me that God was going to use me to restore my family. So, now I understood that it was all for His good. It was for my good. In 1 Corinthians 15:54–55, sin brought about a separation, but salvation brought about unity, restoration, and redemption. As a leaders, we must give an account. We must sense that what we do matters to God. Only then will we feel deep satisfaction for our "work.

From the Pew to the Pulpit
Tyrone Pickett

And now, I walk not just as a man, but as a man on mission. Not a mission of ego or ambition, but one forged in the fire of surrender. The tearing down of pride, rejection, hatred, and unforgiveness was not a loss—it was a liberation. In their place, God planted humility, grace, love, and healing.

This mission is not just about preaching sermons or leading services. It's about restoring what was broken, rebuilding what was lost, and redeeming what was scarred. It's about being the priest of my home, the anchor for my family, and the vessel through which God's glory can flow.

I now understand that every trial, every tear, and every test was preparation. God wasn't just calling me to ministry—He was calling me to maturity. To integrity. To legacy. And as I continue to walk this path, I do so with the conviction that my life matters to God. My mission matters to God. And because of that, I will not quit. I will not fold. I will not retreat.

I am a man on a mission—and that mission is to reflect Christ, restore my family, and release the Kingdom.

Chapter 8: Recognize the Potential

Jeremiah 1:4-7a (ESV) says, "Now the word of the Lord came to me, saying, 'Before I formed you in the womb I knew you, and before you were born, I consecrated you; I appointed you a prophet to the nations.' Then I said, 'Ah, Lord God! Behold, I do not know how to speak, for I am only a youth.' But the Lord said to me, 'Do not say, 'I am only a youth';..."

Definition of recognize: (find someone or something) from having met them before, know again. Acknowledge the existence, validity, or legality of.

Define potential: having or showing the ability to become or develop into something in the future. Latent qualities or abilities that may be developed and lead to the future success or usefulness.

Romans 8:28 (NKJV) says, "And we know that all things work together for good to those who love God, to those who are called according to His purpose."

Psalm 119:9-10 (ESV) says, "How can a young man keep his way pure? By guarding it according to your word. With my whole heart I seek you; let me not wander from your commandments!"

From the Pew to the Pulpit
Tyrone Pickett

I now recognize that my calling was never about my age, my background, or my perceived limitations—it was about God's foreknowledge and His divine appointment. Before I ever took my first breath, He had already spoken purpose over my life. Before I ever doubted myself, He had already declared my potential. Like Jeremiah, I once questioned my readiness. I once wrestled with insecurity, wondering if I had the voice, the strength, or the wisdom to carry the weight of what God was asking. But God silenced my excuses with His Word. He reminded me that purity begins with pursuit, and purpose begins with surrender.

I've come to understand that potential is not just what lies ahead—it's what God has already placed within. And when I align my heart with His commandments, when I seek Him with my whole heart, I unlock the future He's already written.

So, I stand, not in perfection, but in pursuit. Not in fear, but in faith. Because I know now that all things—every struggle, every setback, every scar—are working together for my good. I am called. I am consecrated. I am appointed. And I will walk boldly in the mission He has set before me.

From the Pew to the Pulpit
Tyrone Pickett

Final Chapter: From Glory to Legacy

As I reflect on the path God carved for me—from the pain of rejection to the power of restoration—I now see that every detour, delay, and disappointment was a divine setup. What once felt like abandonment was actually alignment. What once felt like brokenness was the birthplace of boldness. And what once felt like silence was God's sovereign whisper preparing me for the pulpit.

I've learned that ministry is not a destination—it's a daily decision. A decision to love when it hurts. To lead when it's lonely. To serve when it's sacrificial. And to trust when the vision seems bigger than the vessel.

But this story isn't just mine. It's a blueprint for every believer who's ever felt overlooked, underqualified, or unworthy. If God can take a breech-born boy, pronounced dead, raised in obscurity, and turn him into an Apostle, then He can do the same for you. Because the pew is not your prison—it's your preparation.

Now, I live not just for the pulpit, but for the legacy. For the sons and daughters, the spiritual grandchildren, the churches, and the communities that will rise because someone dared to believe that God's plan was greater than man's pain.

So, I close this book not with a period, but with a comma—because the story continues. In every sermon preached, every soul reached, and every life transformed. *From the pew to the pulpit...to the promise.*

To God be the glory.
The best is still unfolding.

www.ingramcontent.com/pod-product-compliance
Lightning Source LLC
LaVergne TN
LVHW051513070426
835507LV00022B/3079